"I love the way that the author keeps language simple and incorporates visuals for each explanation. The accessible layout will make it possible to navigate even on a worst, most anxious day. Images may even be stored and collated in memory and associated with situations as they arise. I love the use of examples of others who might experience the same things and the way key questions allow an opportunity for self-reflection, discussion and awareness. This book is a brilliant concept and I'm certain it will be a really useful resource."

– Adele Devine, author, special needs teacher and co-Founder of the multi-award-winning SEN Assist autism software

"Joel's newest book presents readers with fantastic visuals that provide an accessible approach to the physical and emotional stages of regulation, but, more importantly, it also includes practical strategies that allow for children to feel in control throughout their day."

– Lauren Brukner, Occupational Therapist and author of the Awesome and In Control *Series*

"By following Joel's expert advice, children will learn how to replace their emotional flip switch with a more disciplined dimmer switch. Now that would certainly be something to feel better about!"

– K.I. Al-Ghani, Specialist Advisory Teacher, University Lecturer, Autism Trainer and international author of books on ASD

THE ASD FEEL BETTER BOOK

by the same author

The Conversation Train
A Visual Approach to Conversation for
Children on the Autism Spectrum
ISBN 978 1 84905 986 2
eISBN 978 0 85700 900 5

The Green Zone Conversation Book
Finding Common Ground in Conversation
for Children on the Autism Spectrum
ISBN 978 1 84905 759 2
eISBN 978 0 85700 946 3

Our Brains are Like Computers!
Exploring Social Skills and Social Cause and Effect
with Children on the Autism Spectrum
ISBN 978 1 84905 716 5
eISBN 978 1 78450 208 9

The ASD and Me Picture Book
A Visual Guide to Understanding Challenges and
Strengths for Children on the Autism Spectrum
ISBN 978 1 78592 723 2
eISBN 978 1 78450 351 2

of related interest

Stay Cool and In Control with the Keep Calm Guru
Wise Ways for Children to Regulate
their Emotions and Senses
Lauren Brukner
Illustrated by Apsley
ISBN 978 1 78592 714 0
eISBN 978 1 78450 300 0

The Kids' Guide to Staying Awesome and In Control
Simple Stuff to Help Children Regulate
their Emotions and Senses
Lauren Brukner
ISBN 978 1 84905 997 8
eISBN 978 0 85700 962 3

Becoming a STAR Detective!
Your Detective's Notebook for Finding Clues to How You Feel
Susan Young
ISBN 978 1 78592 180 3
eISBN 978 1 78450 452 6

THE ASD FEEL BETTER BOOK

A VISUAL GUIDE TO HELP BRAIN AND BODY FOR CHILDREN ON THE AUTISM SPECTRUM

JOEL SHAUL

Jessica Kingsley Publishers
London and Philadelphia

First published in 2018
by Jessica Kingsley Publishers
73 Collier Street
London N1 9BE, UK
and
400 Market Street, Suite 400
Philadelphia, PA 19106, USA

www.jkp.com

Library of Congress Cataloging in Publication Data
A CIP catalog record for this book is available from the Library of Congress

British Library Cataloguing in Publication Data
A CIP catalogue record for this book is available from the British Library

ISBN 978 1 78592 762 1
eISBN 978 1 78450 627 8

Printed and bound in China

CONTENTS

INTRODUCTION

When we feel bad, we all do whatever we can to feel better again. But so often, the various ways we feel bad – anxiety, anger, sadness, sensory discomfort – affect our ability to help ourselves. As we go through life, we try to work out solutions in advance, so that when we urgently need to feel better we know what to do.

All children need help learning how to help themselves. Children on the autism spectrum need even more help, since they face special challenges in learning self-help skills. First, with their tendency to focus on a limited range of comforting activities, children on the spectrum are often reluctant to try unfamiliar self-help measures that might be beneficial to them. In addition, their lives are in many ways more stressful, and often children on the spectrum find it hard to monitor the inner states that affect well-being. Often, at the times children with ASD are experiencing high levels of emotional or sensory distress, their problem-solving capacity is at its lowest.

The ASD Feel Better Book is designed to help children on the autism spectrum to develop insight into what makes them feel bad and then increase their awareness of how to make themselves feel good again. The book proceeds through various components of the mind and body to isolate what can go wrong and then explores the measures that are available to make things better.

Suggestions on how to use the book

The book is designed to be read with an adult with frequent pauses for problem-solving exercises and skills practice. Emphasize the parts of the book that seem to be most important for the child you are working with. "The Feel Better Idea Finder" on page 76 is useful to photocopy and keep on hand right from the start as you work through the chapters in the book. The Learning Activities in Part 7 are not mandatory – look them over and pick out the ones that best suit the needs and interests of the child you are helping.

PART 1

FEELING GOOD AND FEELING BAD

In life, everyone has problems to figure out.

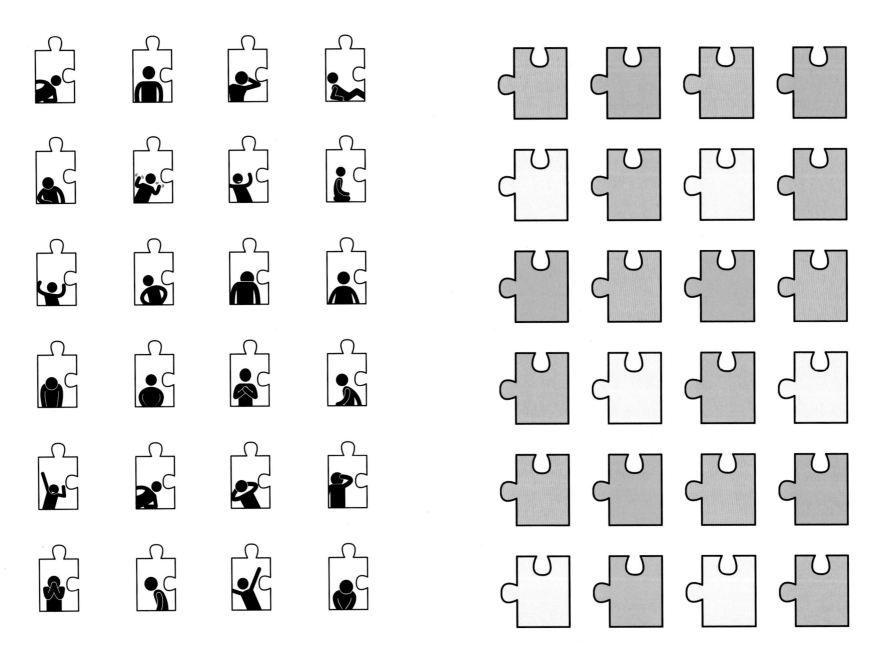

Sometimes the answer to a problem is pretty easy.

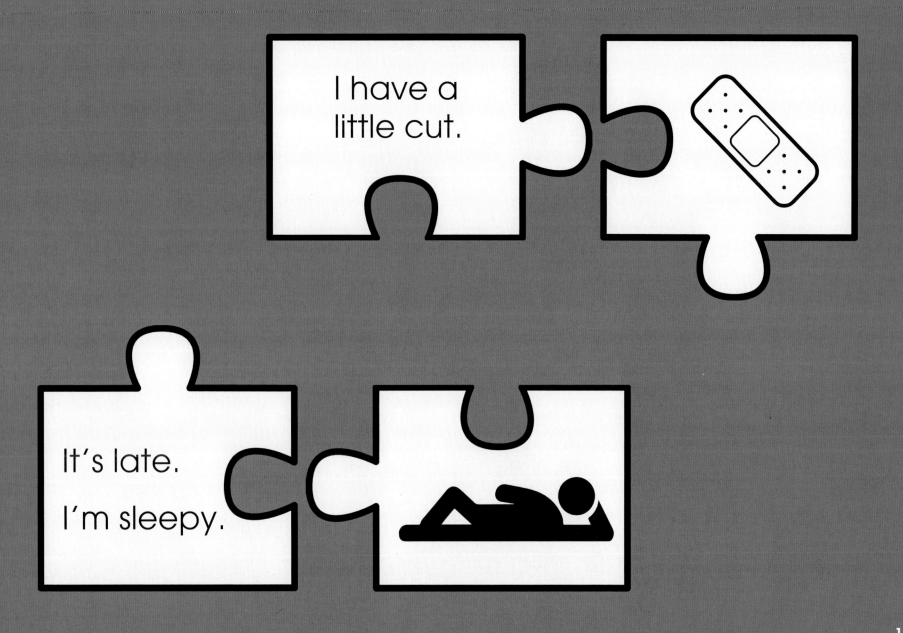

But quite often, feeling unhappy can make it so hard to think.

THEN, IT IS HARD TO FIGURE OUT HOW TO FEEL BETTER.

Sunday afternoon at home and I'm hyper and bored.

New teacher tomorrow and I'm so WORRIED!

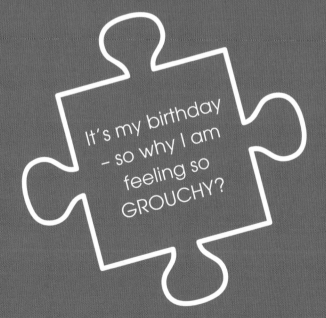

It's my birthday – so why I am feeling so GROUCHY?

Life can be hard.

No one can feel good all of the time. Sometimes it is normal to feel bad.

Usually, though, we can make ourselves feel better.

WE DO THIS BY CHANGING A GREAT MANY THINGS
WE DO - ALL OVER THE BODY AND MIND.

PART 2

GIVING YOUR BODY WHAT IT NEEDS

When we are very young, grown-ups do everything for us to make us feel better.

With the help of adults, we begin to learn how to help ourselves when we have a problem.

As we get older, we can learn to fix more and more of our problems on our own.

There are many ways your body can feel good.

HERE ARE A FEW.

RELAXED

ENERGETIC

SAFE

ACTIVE

COZY

EXCITED

17

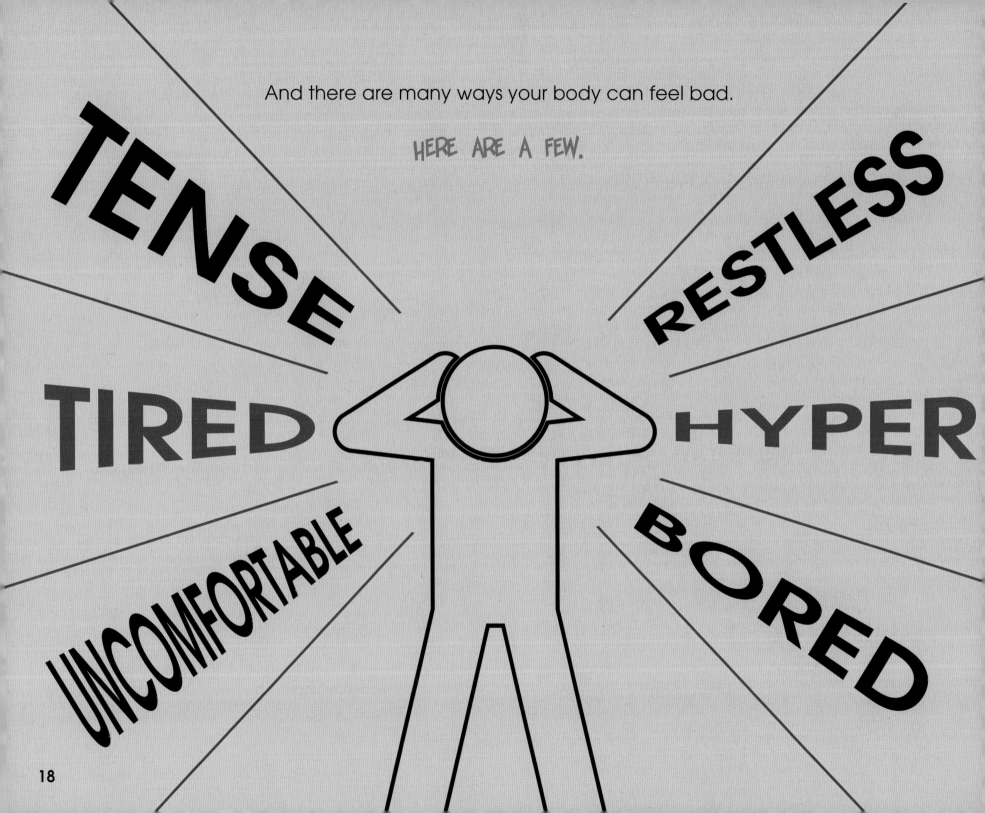

And there are many ways your body can feel bad.

HERE ARE A FEW.

TENSE

RESTLESS

TIRED

HYPER

UNCOMFORTABLE

BORED

18

Often, when you don't feel quite right, it's because your body needs something.

THERE ARE A GREAT MANY THINGS YOUR BODY MIGHT NEED.

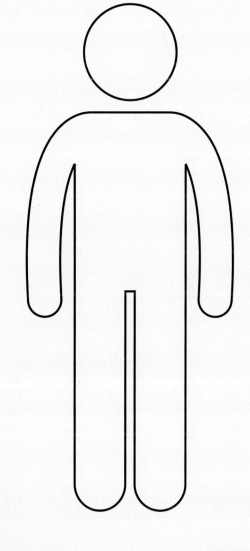

Stretch

Go outside

Play

Get a drink

Eat healthy

Sleep

Exercise

Lie down

Sit down

SOMETIMES, YOUR BODY NEEDS TO MOVE AROUND, STRETCH AND USE UP SOME ENERGY.

Your body might need to exercise. Everyone needs to move around and make their body feel tired.

What are the main ways that you get exercise?

The inside of your body can get tight and tense and this can make you feel bad. There are many different ways to stretch out your arms, legs and other parts of your body.

Do you know how to stretch?

Exercise

Stretch

Josh's body is feeling restless because he's been using his computer for five hours. He feels better after playing with his sister outside for a while.

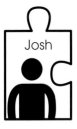
Josh

Go outside

Play

Brian is full of energy but it is raining outside and he doesn't know what to do. His dad has him spend some time on the treadmill and then they both do stretching together.

Brian

Stretch

Exercise

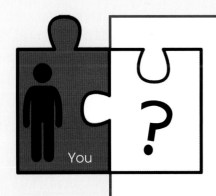
You

When does your body get restless and full of energy?

What are some things you can do to feel better and calmer?

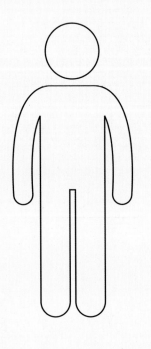

THERE ARE TIMES AND PLACES WHEN DOING JUST WHAT YOUR BODY WANTS IS OKAY.

Some people's bodies have a strong need to move in some special or unusual ways. There is a special word for this: "stimming."

If your body feels good when you "stim," you can find out from your family and teachers when and where it is okay to move in this way.

Move the way you want

Jasmine always tries hard in school but at least once a day her body wants to "stim" a lot. After Jasmine's work is finished, she is allowed to go to the back of the room and move around till she feels better. Jasmine paces back and forth and flaps her arms.

Jasmine

Move the way you want

On weekends at home, energy builds up in Omar until he starts running around the house, humming to himself. Omar's dad shows him how to use a mini-trampoline and a treadmill when he feels the need to stim.

Omar

Move the way you want

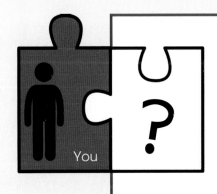

You

What about you? Does your body ever need to "stim," to move in certain ways over and over for you to feel good?

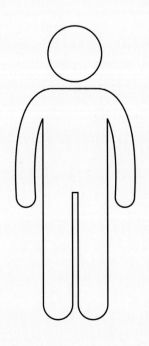

SOMETIMES, YOUR BODY IS TIRED AND NEEDS REST.

The energy in different parts of your body needs to recharge.

There are different kinds of rest that you can do in different places and at different times.

When is a time for you sit down to rest?	When are times you can lie down?	When are times you can sleep?
Sit down	**Lie down**	**Sleep**

At her after-school program, Karen really wants to play. But she realizes she is getting very tired. She sits down, then asks one of the workers if she can lie down for a while.

Karen

Sit down

Lie down

Tyler is getting grouchy during school today. It takes weeks for Tyler and his dad to figure out the problem – he is watching videos on his phone way past his bedtime. Tyler's dad now keeps the phone at bedtime, and Tyler is less tired at school. He is in a better mood too.

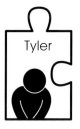

Tyler

Sleep

You

When do you notice that your body is getting tired or sleepy?

When do you need to rest more?

When do you need to sleep more?

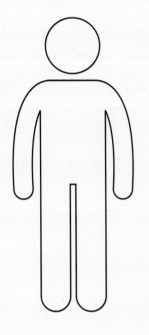

SOMETIMES, YOUR BODY
NEEDS WATER OR FOOD.

Your body needs water and
food for it to keep going.

The right foods at the right
times can make your body
feel good and strong.

Get a drink

Eat healthy

When Justin feels thirsty, his mom gives him juice to drink. He loves the taste and how it makes him feel good and full. At his grandmother's house, Justin begs for juice but he is usually just given water instead. Justin's doctor says that once or twice a day is enough juice for Justin.

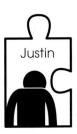

Justin

Get a drink

Ted eats a good breakfast before school and feels hungry again by about 10 a.m. His old teacher used to give out cookies at this time, but the new teacher passes out grapes and carrots. Ted is trying to get used to this new snack. The new teacher says this kind of food is healthy and gives people more energy.

Ted

Eat healthy

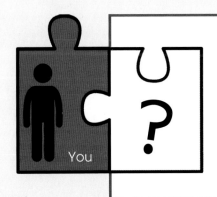

You

What about you?

Have you, or adults, ever tried to change what you are given to drink or eat so that it is better for your body?

To help make the rest of you feel good, your hands might need to be busy getting something done.

Your hands might need to:

- draw or write

- put something together

- play a game

- play an instrument

Your hands have other needs too. Often, when your hands feel good, the rest of you feels better too.

Your hands might want to hold or touch:

- something smooth, or rough

- something hard, or squishy

Busy working hands

Hold or touch something that feels good

Tom is in the back seat on a long car ride. He is bored playing with his tablet and his hands feel restless. He plays with modeling clay. Later, he finds that holding his sister's bear feels good. Later, he pets the dog.

Tom

Hold or touch something that feels good

On Sunday, Carlos wakes up feeling hyper. In his home, he is pacing around touching things and kind of annoying people. Carlos remembers the drawing of a dragon that he had started yesterday. As he works on it, he is calmer and it feels good to have his hands busy.

Carlos

Busy working hands

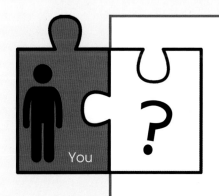

You

When your hands are restless and they need something to do, what kinds of activities make them feel better?

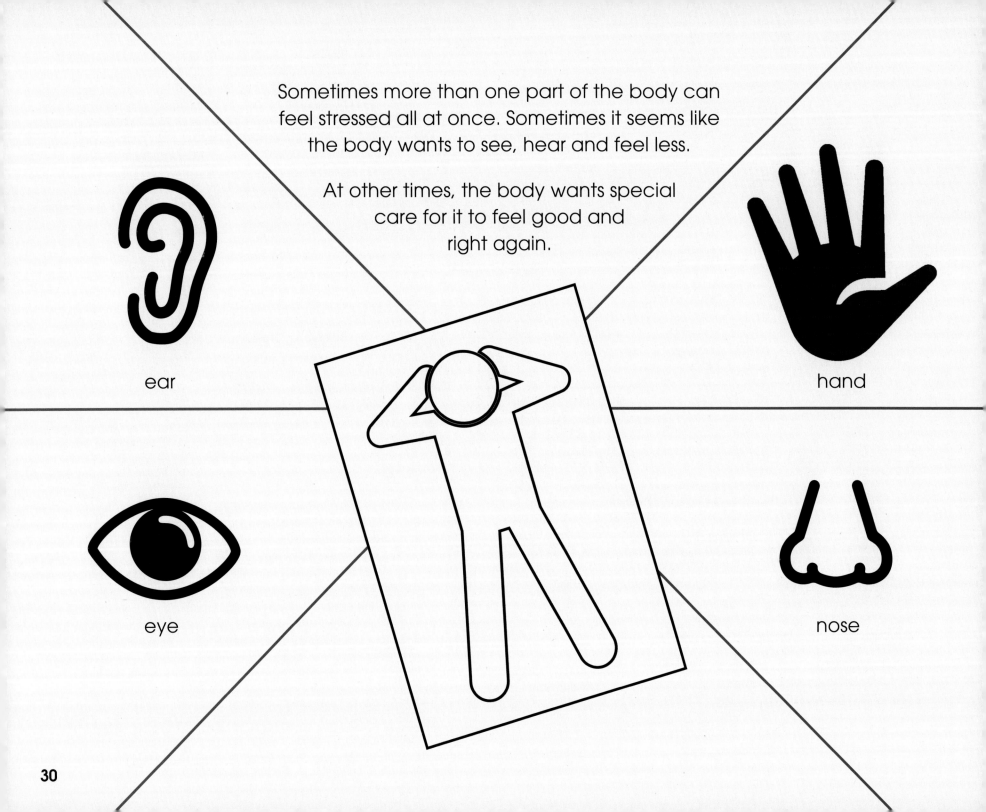

Sometimes more than one part of the body can feel stressed all at once. Sometimes it seems like the body wants to see, hear and feel less.

At other times, the body wants special care for it to feel good and right again.

ear

hand

eye

nose

Your arms, legs or other parts of your body might want to be squeezed, covered up or pressed down upon.

Get hugged or squeezed

Weight pressing down on you

Hold yourself

At other times, parts of your body might want a break from seeing, hearing and feeling things.

Ask for help

Can you please help me?

Cozy, closed-in place

Find quiet

Cover up

Listen to music

On Saturday, Jared's body does not feel right and nothing seems to help. Then he knows what to do. He tells his mom he is going to his room. When he gets there, he covers himself with a heavy blanket and puts on his headphones.

 Jared Weight pressing down on you Cover up Listen to music

Kyla feels anxious. She tries hugging herself for a while but it is not enough. She asks her grandmother to hug her while they sit together. Then, Kyla settles into the corner with a book until she feels better.

 Kyla Hold yourself Get hugged or squeezed Cozy, closed-in place

Sam has been trying to get used to the lunchroom. First, he tries using different kinds of ear protection to deal with the noise. Then he finds out that sometimes students can ask to go down to the library after they are done eating. The quiet in the library feels great to Sam.

 Sam Find quiet Ask for a break — Can I have a break, please?

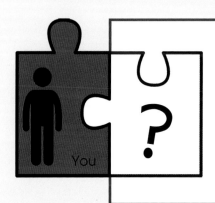

Does your body need to feel squeezed or covered up sometimes?

Do you need to be alone in a quiet place to calm down?

Weight pressing down on you

Cover up

Listen to music

Hold yourself

Get hugged or squeezed

Cozy, closed-in place

Find quiet

Ask for a break

Can I have a break, please?

Everyone is different. What are the main things you need to do for your body so you can feel good? Which things do you do already? Which ones do you need to do more?

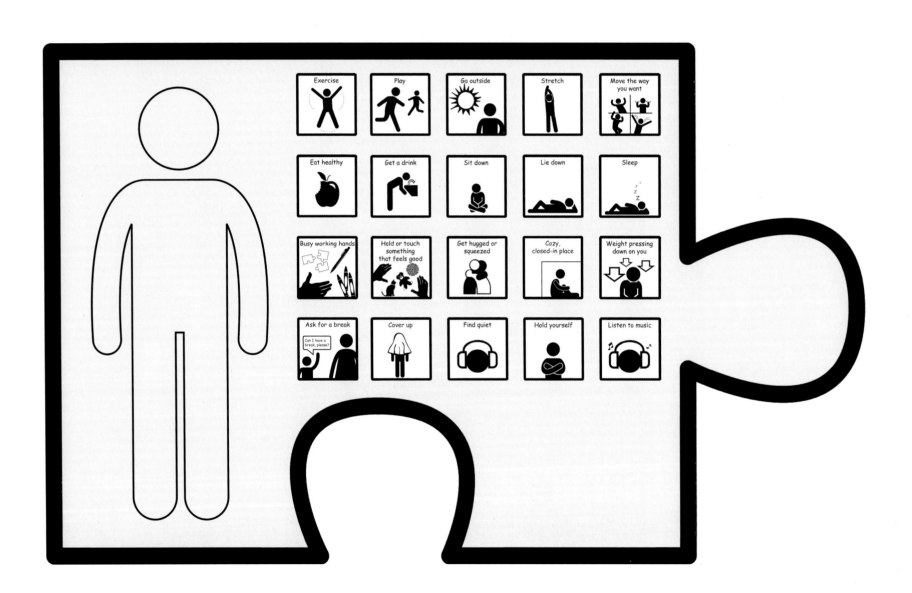

PART 3

GIVING YOUR BREATHING WHAT IT NEEDS

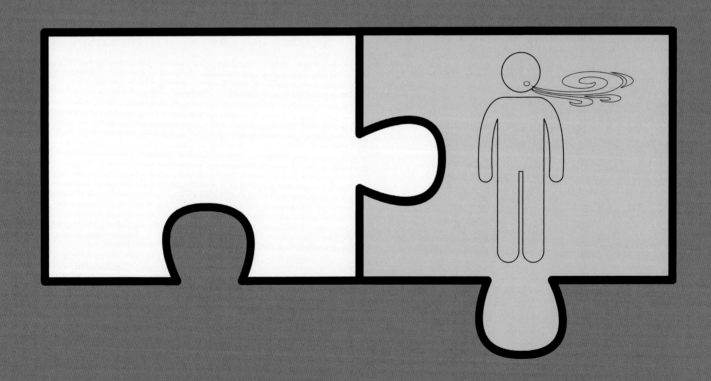

The way you breathe is important.

Certain ways of breathing can make you feel good. Other ways can make you feel bad.

To feel really good, you need to take care of the part of you that does breathing – your lungs.

Give the lungs good exercise

Relaxation breathing

The lungs

You have probably noticed how your breathing can get heavy and uncomfortable when you are unhappy.

Here is how that happens.

When you feel really worried, angry or upset, your brain sometimes tells your breathing to speed up.

Lungs! Go FASTER!

But then, the breathing starts going *too* fast! And this can make your brain and your body feel even more worried, angry and upset than before.

When you calm down your breathing, your lungs tell your brain that things are alright.

This can make you feel much better.

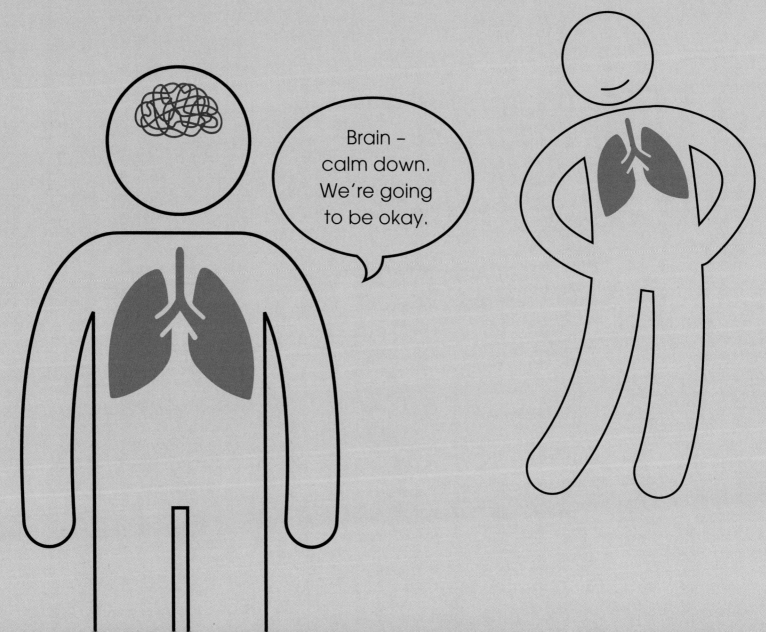

Sometimes, people aren't used to getting "out of breath," but it is really good to do this through exercising. If you have been sitting or lying down too much and then you play a lot or exercise, your lungs need to work hard for a while to move a lot of air in and out. Then, the rest of your body can feel more relaxed.

We can practice a special way to breathe, called relaxation breathing. This can really help us feel relaxed and calm.

Give the lungs good exercise

Relaxation breathing

In the lunchroom at school, Jim notices a tightness in his chest that does not feel good. During recess, right after lunch, he runs as fast as he can for a while and he breathes very hard. The tight feeling goes away.

Jim

Give the lungs good exercise

Nina is sitting in the back seat of the car on the way to a recital, where she will play her violin in front of lots of people. She tells her mother she is worried that she will play her instrument poorly. Nina and her mother do some relaxation breathing and then Nina feels a little better.

Nina

Relaxation breathing

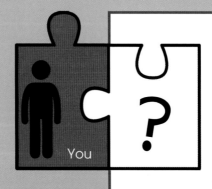

You

When do you notice that your breathing does not feel right?

Have you tried relaxation breathing to help your breathing to feel better?

1

Take a deep, slow breath. Hold it in for a second or two.

2

Breathe out slowly over 3 or 4 seconds.

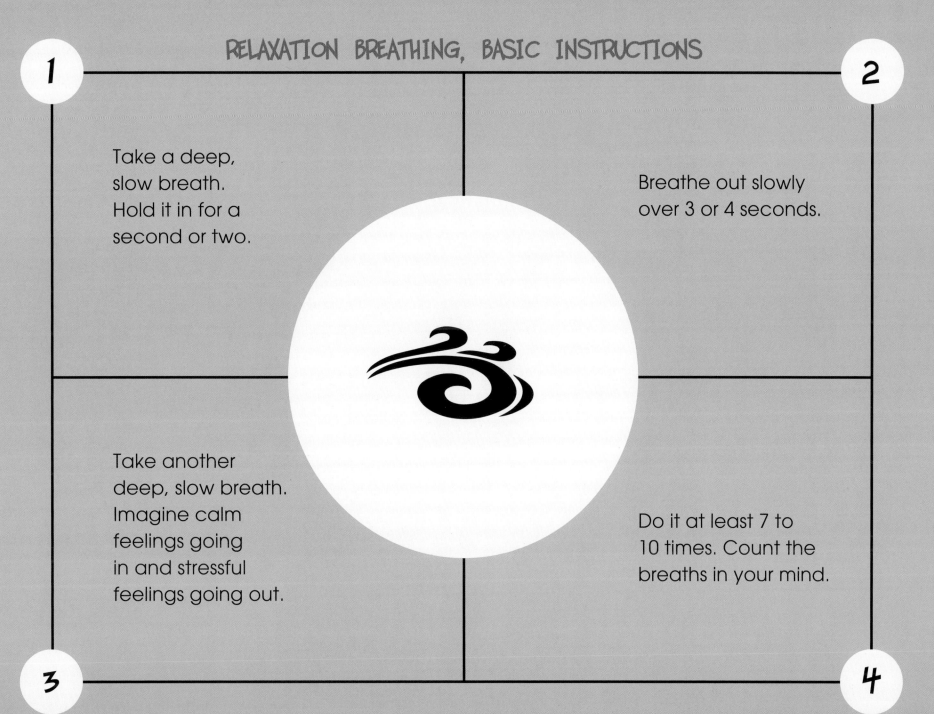

3

Take another deep, slow breath. Imagine calm feelings going in and stressful feelings going out.

4

Do it at least 7 to 10 times. Count the breaths in your mind.

When are some times that you could give your lungs good exercise?

When are some times that you could use relaxation breathing to help you to feel calmer?

PART 4

GIVING YOUR MIND WHAT IT NEEDS

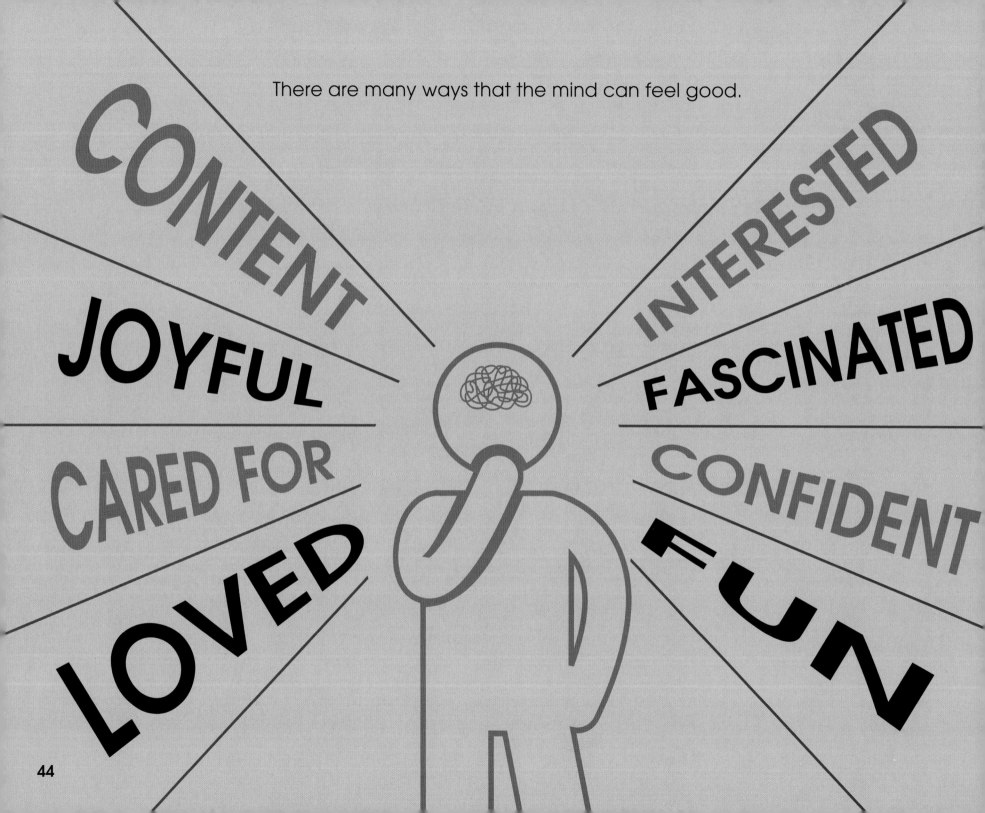

There are many ways that the mind can feel good.

CONTENT

INTERESTED

JOYFUL

FASCINATED

CARED FOR

CONFIDENT

LOVED

FUN

44

And there are so many different ways to feel bad!

ANGRY

SAD

DISAPPOINTED

FRUSTRATED

WORRIED

CONFUSED

LONELY

ASHAMED

Whether we feel good, bad or in between, it has a lot to do with our thoughts, and what we do with our minds.

Our minds are busy places, where we are always having thoughts.

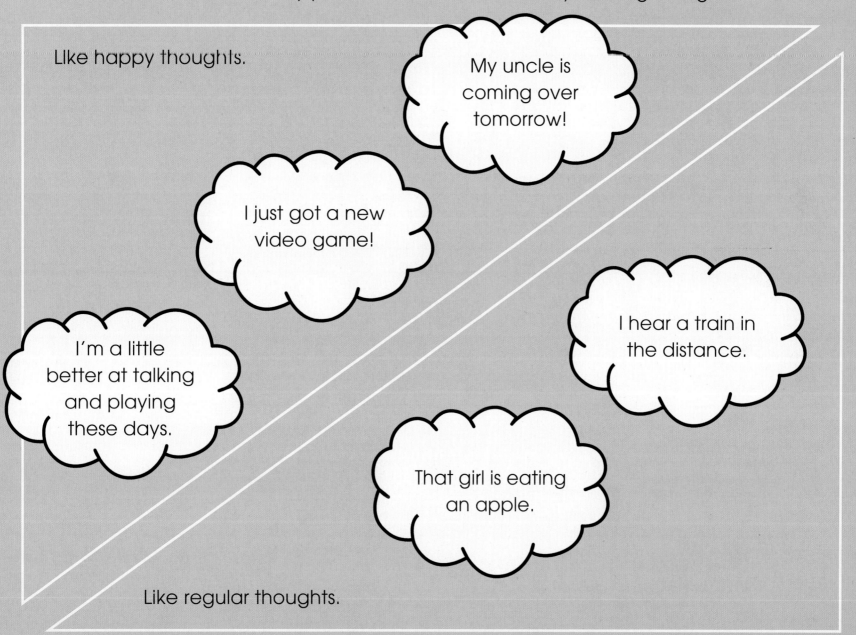

Like happy thoughts.

My uncle is coming over tomorrow!

I just got a new video game!

I hear a train in the distance.

I'm a little better at talking and playing these days.

That girl is eating an apple.

Like regular thoughts.

When positive thoughts are stronger than other thoughts, we feel better.

When negative thoughts are stronger than other thoughts, we feel worse.

That new kid smiled at me and said hello. Maybe he likes me.

Maybe we can hang out together at recess.

I'm a little better at talking and playing these days.

Other kids will tell the new guy that I'm weird.

The new guy will like the other kids more than me.

I should go play by myself like usual, so my feelings don't get hurt.

There are many ways to make
our positive thoughts stronger.

One way to make positive thoughts stronger is
to give the mind good things to think about.

Give your brain something else to do

Look forward to something nice

Think of something funny

As she is getting ready for bed, Maria cannot stop thinking about her gym class the next day and how much she hates it. She makes herself think about the nice weekend coming up in two days. This makes her thoughts about gym seem not quite as awful.

Maria

Look forward to something nice

Jeremy's friend just got a new video game system – the same one that Jeremy has wanted for a year and which his parents will not buy for him. Jeremy's mind gets stuck on jealous and angry thoughts. Jeremy makes up his mind to move on to something else. He reads a comic book and then watches a funny video.

Jeremy

Give your brain something else to do

Think of something funny

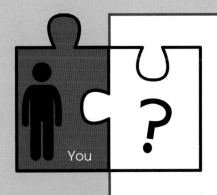

You

When do you notice that your own mind is getting stuck on something unhappy?

What kinds of things can you do to get your mind to move on to something else?

There are other times when we can teach our mind to focus in special ways to help it to relax.

Think of a relaxing place

Meditate

As Kara is about to fall asleep in her bed, she can just barely hear her parents talking in another room. Are they talking about how they might have to move again because of Dad's job? Now Kara feels upset! She makes her mind think about a special chair she likes to sit at in the library. Her mind starts to relax.

Kara

Think of a relaxing place

More and more these days, Ian's mind can't calm down. As soon as he gets rid of one worry, another one replaces it. Ian's counselor has been teaching him how to meditate. He teaches Ian how to clear his mind and have quiet thoughts. Ian tries it at home. It is hard at first but he seems to be getting better at it.

Ian

Meditate

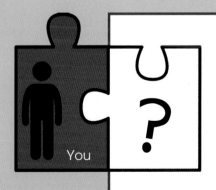

You

When you need to focus your mind on a "happy place," a peaceful place that calms you down, what do you think of?

There are many ways to calm and focus your thoughts. This is called meditation. Have you tried this? Do you know anyone who could help you to do it better?

Another way of fixing our thoughts is very important. It takes practice to learn.

We can pay special attention to certain kinds of upsetting thoughts. Then, we can fight against them and replace them with different thoughts.

Find the upsetting thoughts

Think: This problem will pass

Try better thoughts

After David fell and broke his leg, he did okay with the visit to the doctor and getting the cast put on. At first, David feels terribly discouraged when he finds out that the cast would have to stay on his leg for six weeks. Then David tells himself, "It's six weeks. Not a lifetime. I will get through this."

David

Think: This problem will pass

Quinn tries and tries to get to the next level in his video game, but he fails. His mind fills up with negative thoughts. "You're a loser. It's not just video games; you mess up everything!" Quinn puts down the video game and takes a walk. He looks for new thoughts that will fight against the bad thoughts.

Quinn

Find the upsetting thoughts

Try better thoughts

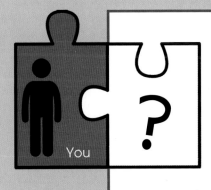

You

When have you noticed that your own mind is getting stuck on something that is making you unhappy?

What kinds of things can you do to get your mind to move on to something else?

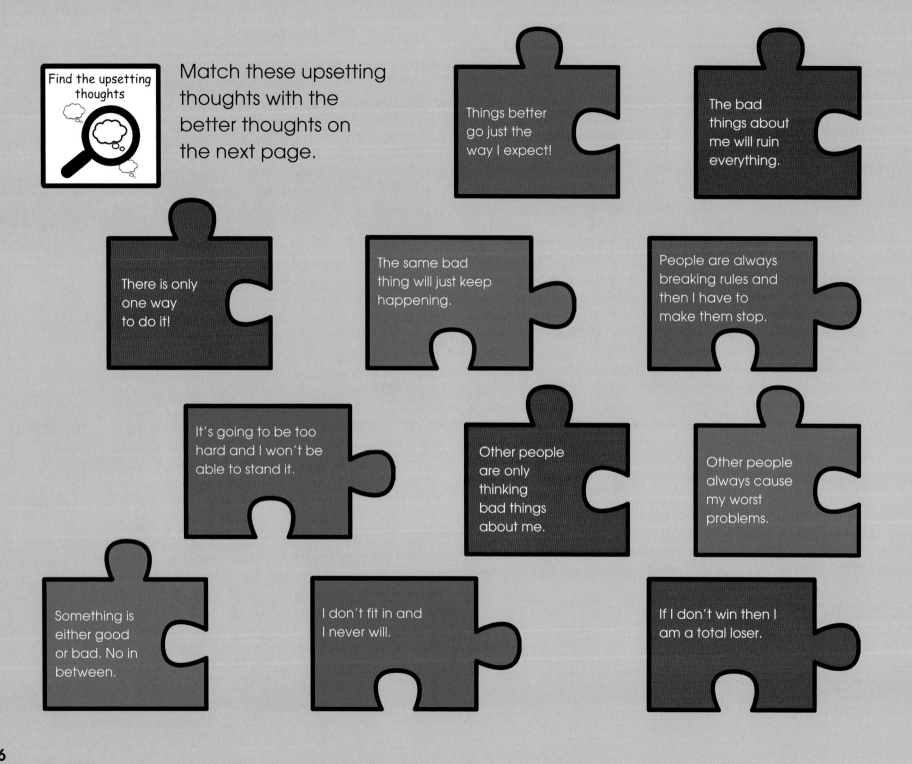

Find the upsetting thoughts

Match these upsetting thoughts with the better thoughts on the next page.

Things better go just the way I expect!

The bad things about me will ruin everything.

There is only one way to do it!

The same bad thing will just keep happening.

People are always breaking rules and then I have to make them stop.

It's going to be too hard and I won't be able to stand it.

Other people are only thinking bad things about me.

Other people always cause my worst problems.

Something is either good or bad. No in between.

I don't fit in and I never will.

If I don't win then I am a total loser.

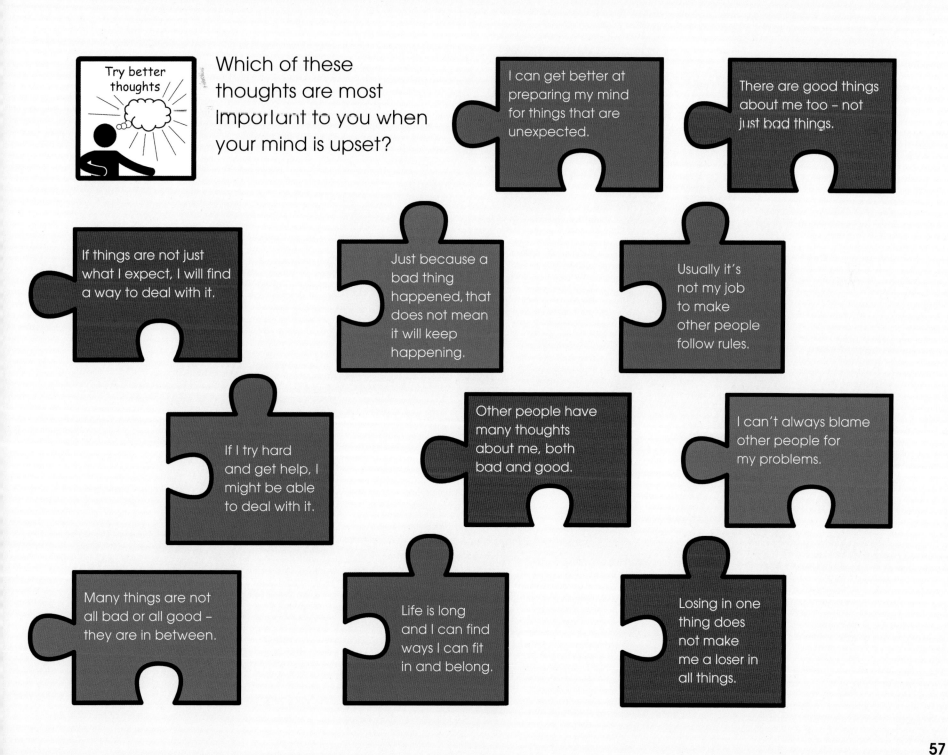

Which of these thoughts are most Important to you when your mind is upset?

Try better thoughts

I can get better at preparing my mind for things that are unexpected.

There are good things about me too – not just bad things.

If things are not just what I expect, I will find a way to deal with it.

Just because a bad thing happened, that does not mean it will keep happening.

Usually it's not my job to make other people follow rules.

If I try hard and get help, I might be able to deal with it.

Other people have many thoughts about me, both bad and good.

I can't always blame other people for my problems.

Many things are not all bad or all good – they are in between.

Life is long and I can find ways I can fit in and belong.

Losing in one thing does not make me a loser in all things.

USING OUR OWN BRAINS – AND OTHER PEOPLE'S BRAINS – TO GET HELP.

Because we live inside our own bodies and think with our own brains, we often can figure out, on our own, what our bodies and minds need.

I'm too full.

Next time just one of those big donuts – not two.

I feel lonely and restless. Better ask my friend if she wants to hang out this weekend.

At other times, people need other people's thoughts, feelings and ideas to fix a problem.

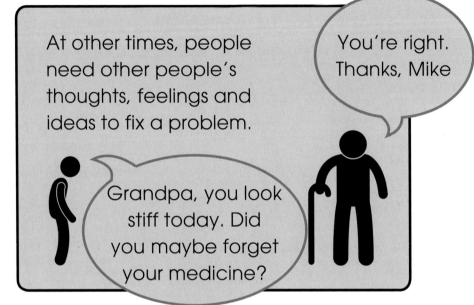

You're right. Thanks, Mike

Grandpa, you look stiff today. Did you maybe forget your medicine?

Mike, you look sad. Want to tell me about it?

Okay, Grandpa.

Ask for help

HERE ARE A FEW EXAMPLES OF PEOPLE YOU CAN USE TO GET ADVICE AND HELP WHEN YOU NEED TO FEEL BETTER.

Get advice

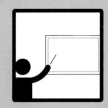

Teachers give you "book learning" but they may also be able to teach you ways to feel better.

Parents and guardians have known you a long time. They often notice your needs before you are aware of them yourself.

A friend might help you to fix a problem, or might get you to play when you are spending too much time alone.

A counselor or therapist has training and experience to help you with special problems so you feel better.

Ava always sat on the bus with Carla. But today Carla sits with Anne instead. Ava can't figure out why her best friend has done this! Ava almost cries, it hurts so bad. At lunch, Ava asks her friend Darlene for advice. Darlene explains that even best friends like to make new friends, and that Ava shouldn't get so upset about it.

Ava

Get advice

Hope has troubling thoughts about herself that just won't go away. First, she tries ignoring them. Hope even asks a friend for advice, but that hardly helps at all. Hope gets up her courage. She decides she will go tell her grandmother everything that is on her mind.

Hope

Ask for help

Can you please help me?

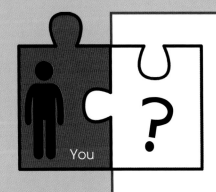

You

Everybody has to get help sometimes. When have you needed to get help with a problem that was really bothering you?

Who are the main people you can go to when you really need help?

It's normal for people to feel bad sometimes. We can't always make ourselves feel as good as we want.

But there are almost always some helpful things we can do in our minds.

What about you?

What are some good things you already do to help your mind? What more do you need to learn?

PART 5

NEEDS VS. WANTS

Sometimes we can get stuck on a few things we use to try to feel better. It feels really good for a while. But in the long run we might get weaker, not stronger.

If we learn how to make ourselves feel better in lots of ways instead of just a few, we can feel even better and be stronger in the long run. We still do the things we like, but just less – and we rely more on the things that are good for us.

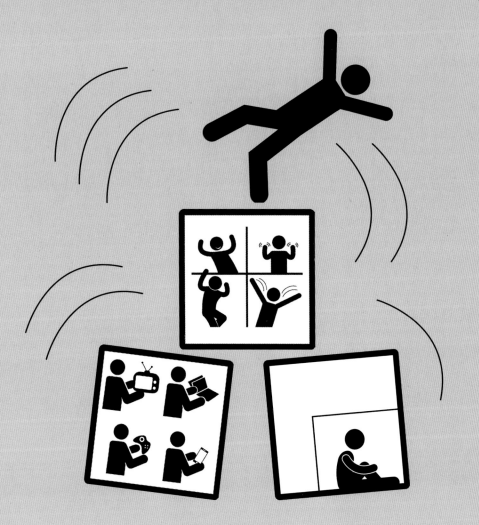

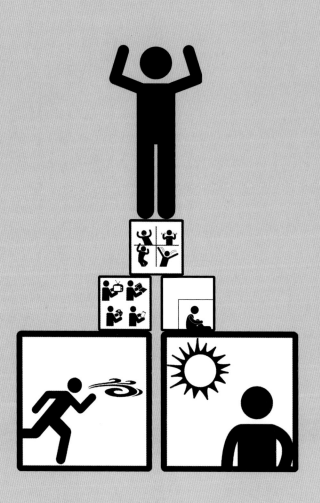

We can think of it like charging and draining batteries in our brains and bodies. The activities shown below are a few that can make our brains and bodies weaker if we do them too much.

Other things we do can seem hard and tiring at first – but they can make us stronger. Even though they might make the mind and body tired at first, they make us much stronger and "recharge our batteries" after we get used to them.

Everyone has to figure out the right mix of activities for them. That way we can feel better and stronger in the long run – instead of just good for a little while.

Below, see some examples of people depending on different things, in different amounts, to feel good.

Who will get stronger? Who will feel good for a while but then get weaker?

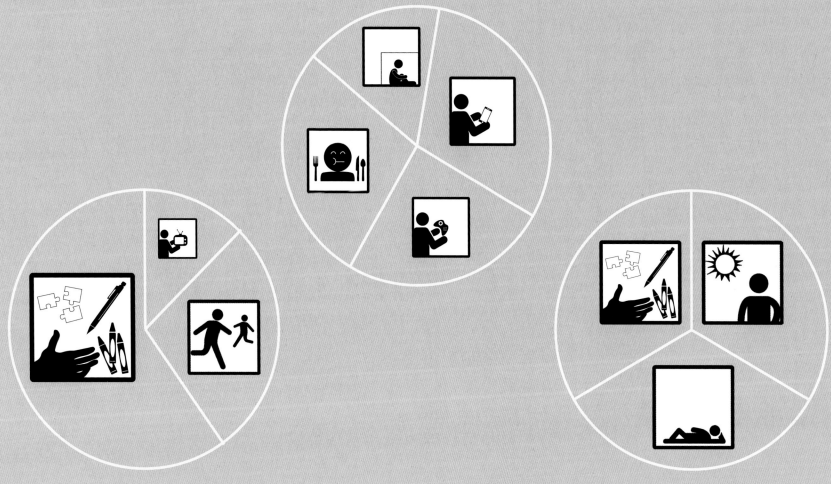

So, some of the most important things we do to feel good are things that might not feel good right away.

These are things we do because they are good for us in the long run, so we can feel better later.

Try to do the hard thing first

Put up with it to make yourself stronger

At his friend's birthday party, Rick is having a hard time with the noise and the crowd. As he picks up his mother's phone to play a game, he feels more relaxed – but he ignores the other children. He is annoyed when his mother takes the phone back, but he eventually joins in with a few children playing a game he kind of likes.

Rick

Try to do the hard thing first

In Jen's gym class, the teacher is having them walk around the track outside. Jen sits down after five minutes and tells the teacher that her legs feel tired. The teacher has Jen get up and walk for ten more minutes. At first this bothers Jen, but after two more gym classes she feels less achy and tired.

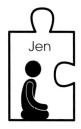

Jen

Put up with it to make yourself stronger

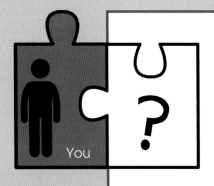

You

What is something difficult that your body has got better at dealing with over time?

What are some hard things you avoid that might make you feel better if you get used to them?

During the first week of her summer day program, Sarah misses her home and her video games terribly. Sarah tries hard to deal with the strange, new ways to play outdoors. By the third week, Sarah still misses playing video games but she is starting to enjoy the summer activities and the kids.

Sarah

Try to do the hard thing first

Kevin and his dad enjoy eating lots of buttered popcorn. The family doctor says they are both getting health problems from being overweight. Kevin's dad starts putting out apples to snack on instead. This is hard for Kevin, but he does look forward to losing some weight and being healthier.

Kevin

Try to do the hard thing first

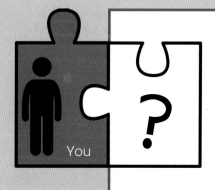

You

Is there any activity, such as playing a game, using a computer or eating, that you have got very stuck on?

Do you really "need" it or do you just want it? Has someone helped you try to cut down on this activity?

What are some things you love that you might do too much or too often?

What are some things that your body and mind really need – things that you should try to do more?

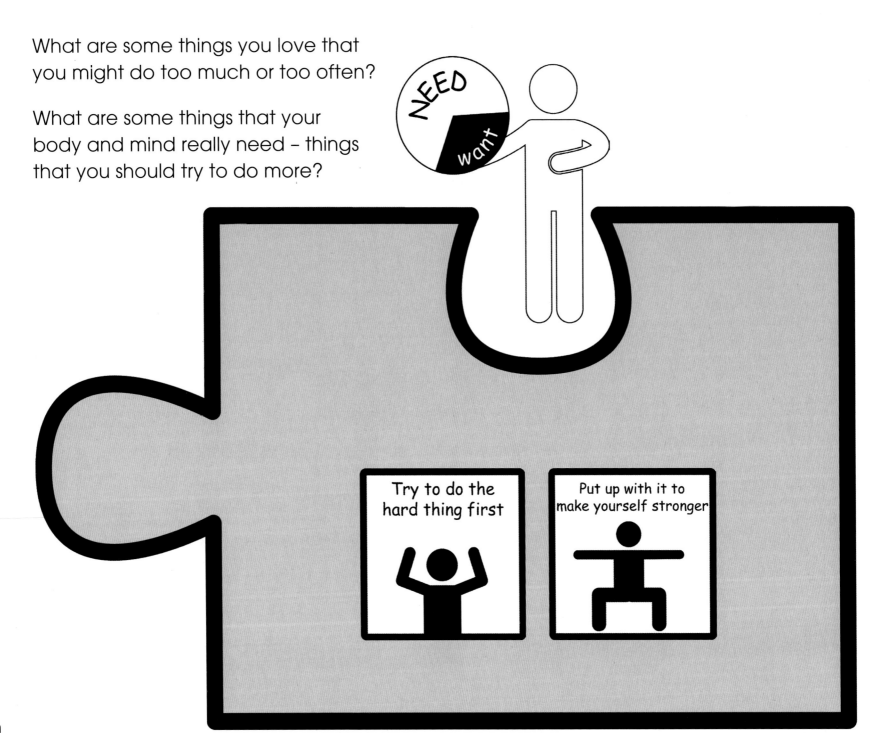

PART 6

PUTTING IT ALL TOGETHER TO FEEL BETTER

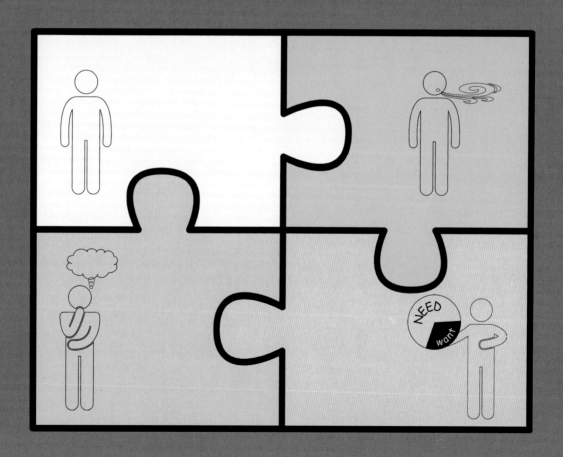

People spend their whole lives figuring out the best ways to feel better.

IT'S TRICKY.

IN THIS BOOK, YOU HAVE LEARNED ABOUT MANY GOOD THINGS TO TRY.

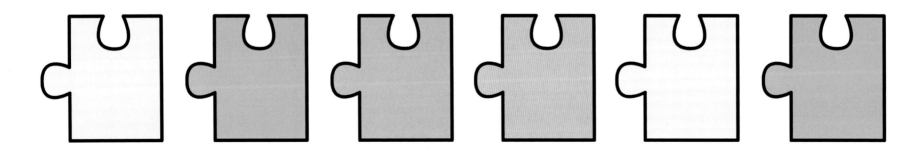

WE ARE ALL DIFFERENT.

PART 7

LEARNING ACTIVITIES

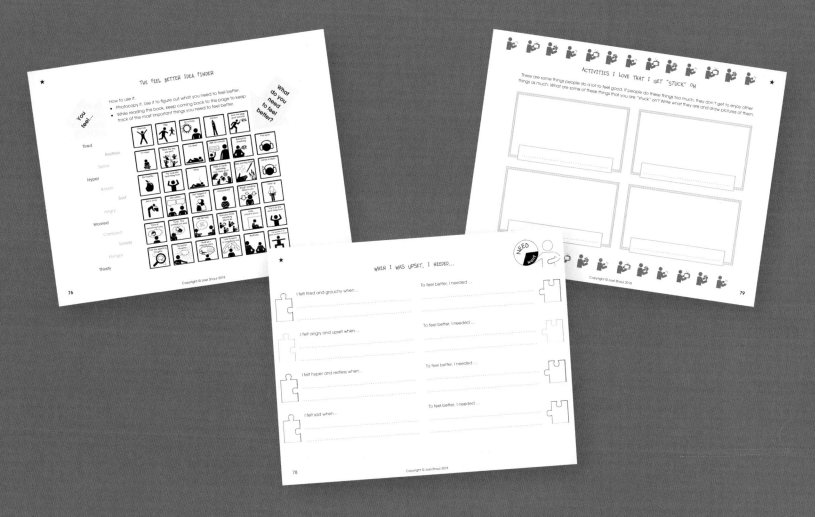

THE FEEL BETTER IDEA FINDER

You feel...

What do you need to feel better?

How to use it:

- Photocopy it. Use it to figure out what you need to feel better.
- While reading this book, keep coming back to this page to keep track of the most important things you need to feel better.

Tired

Restless

Tense

Hyper

Bored

Sad

Angry

Worried

Confused

Lonely

Hungry

Thirsty

Play	Go outside	Stretch	Give the lungs good exercise		
Exercise	Move the way you want	Lie down	Ask for a break	Relaxation breathing	Find quiet
Sit down	Eat healthy	Sleep	Hold or touch something that feels good	Busy working hands	Listen to music
Get a drink	Get advice	Get hugged or squeezed	Hold yourself	Weight pressing down on you	Cover up
Think of something funny	Think: This problem will pass	Ask for help	Give your brain something else to do	Cozy, closed-in place	Try to do the hard thing first
Find the upsetting thoughts	Try better thoughts	Think of a relaxing place	Look forward to something nice	Meditate	Put up with it to make yourself stronger

THE BRAIN AND BODY FEEL BETTER WORKSHEET

Suggestion: Copy "The Feel Better Idea Finder" on page 76 and keep it handy while working on this page.

1 Think about a time you felt very unhappy. Circle the feeling words that describe how you felt at that time.

Tired

Restless

Tense

Hyper

Bored

Sad

Angry

Worried

Confused

Lonely

Other:

. . . .

2 What was making you feel upset?

. . . .
. . . .
. . . .
. . . .
. . . .
. . . .
. . . .
. . . .
. . . .
. . . .
. . . .
. . . .

3 Draw Xs on the parts of your body where you felt the upset feelings.

4 What were some things your brain needed to feel better?

. . . .
. . . .
. . . .
. . . .
. . . .

5 What are some things your body needed to feel better?

. . . .
. . . .
. . . .
. . . .
. . . .

WHEN I WAS UPSET, I NEEDED...

I felt tired and grouchy when...

To feel better, I needed...

....

....

I felt angry and upset when...

To feel better, I needed...

....

....

I felt hyper and restless when...

To feel better, I needed...

....

....

I felt sad when...

To feel better, I needed...

....

....

78

ACTIVITIES I LOVE THAT I GET "STUCK" ON

There are some things people do a lot to feel good. If people do these things too much, they don't get to enjoy other things as much. What are some of these things that you are "stuck" on? Write what they are and draw pictures of them.

79

DIFFERENT ACTIVITIES I MIGHT DO MORE TO FEEL BETTER

When you only do your favorite things you are "stuck" on, you feel good for a while but you might not feel better and stronger in the long run. Pick out some activities you could do more to feel better and stronger.

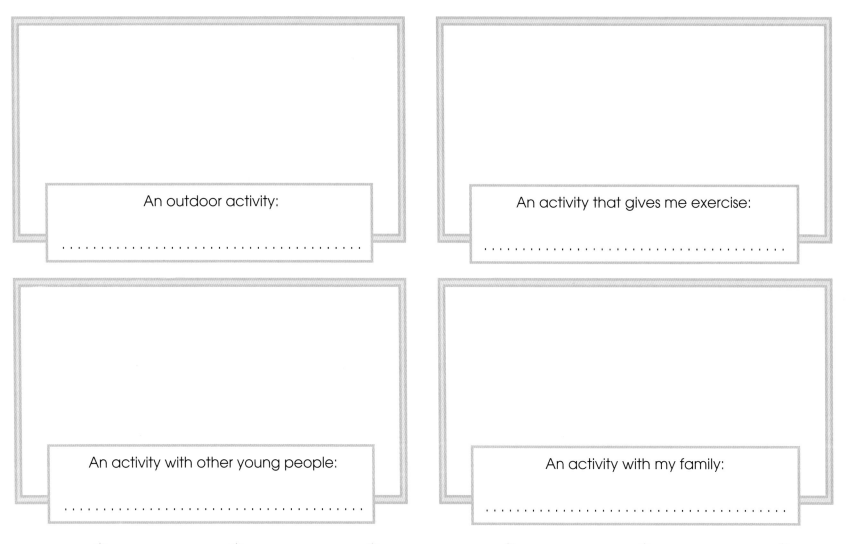

An outdoor activity:

. . . .

An activity that gives me exercise:

. . . .

An activity with other young people:

. . . .

An activity with my family:

. . . .

WHAT I SHOULD KEEP DOING, DO LESS OR DO MORE TO FEEL BETTER

People can feel better and stronger by making some changes in what they do.
Write down some of your own ideas in the three columns below.

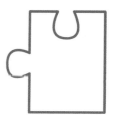

To feel better and stronger, I should **keep doing these things a lot:**	To feel better and stronger, I should **do these things less because they can make me weaker:**	To feel better and stronger, I should **do these things more, even though it might be hard:**

THE FEEL BETTER CHALLENGE GAME

Flip a coin. If you get heads, you must answer one of the squares on the left hand page. If you get tails, you must ask the other player a question from the right hand page.

You can pick the questions in alphabetical order if you like.

THE FEEL BETTER

A Describe a time that feeling upset made you feel different or bad somewhere in your body.

B Which is hardest for you: Anger? Worries? Sadness?

C Describe an outdoor activity that helps you to feel good and relaxed.

D Describe an indoor activity that makes you feel good and relaxed.

E What is something you do with your hands that helps you to feel better?

F Tell about a time that you did an enjoyable thing by yourself for too long.

G Describe what you usually do between waking up and lunchtime on Saturdays.

H Describe what you usually do during the afternoon and evening on Saturdays.

HEADS

ASK YOURSELF!

If you get a heads when you flip the coin, *you must* answer one of the squares on this page.

I Aside from your parents and teachers, who else might help you learn new ways

J Tell about a time that you were able to help someone else feel better when they were upset.

K Describe one feel-good activity you do that you should probably cut down on.

L Of all the ways to feel good taught in this book, name two that seem most important to you.

M Describe a good way to feel better that you learned from a grown-up.

N Describe one ne way to feel goo that you ought try to do more

CHALLENGE GAME

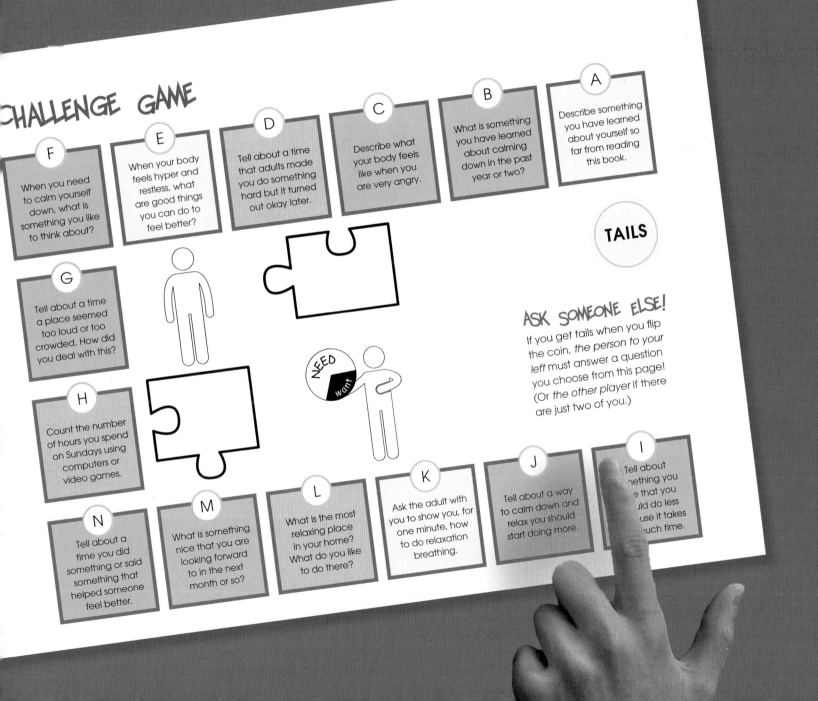

F — When you need to calm yourself down, what is something you like to think about?

E — When your body feels hyper and restless, what are good things you can do to feel better?

D — Tell about a time that adults made you do something hard but it turned out okay later.

C — Describe what your body feels like when you are very angry.

B — What is something you have learned about calming down in the past year or two?

A — Describe something you have learned about yourself so far from reading this book.

G — Tell about a time a place seemed too loud or too crowded. How did you deal with this?

H — Count the number of hours you spend on Sundays using computers or video games.

N — Tell about a time you did or said something or said something that helped someone feel better.

M — What is something nice that you are looking forward to in the next month or so?

L — What is the most relaxing place in your home? What do you like to do there?

K — Ask the adult with you to show you, for one minute, how to do relaxation breathing.

J — Tell about a way to calm down and relax you should start doing more.

I — Tell about ...ething you ...e that you ...uld do less ...use it takes ...uch time.

TAILS

ASK SOMEONE ELSE!

If you get tails when you flip the coin, *the person to your left* must answer a question you choose from this page! (Or *the other player* if there are just two of you.)

NEED / want

THE FEEL BETTER

A Describe a time that feeling upset made you feel different or bad somewhere in your body.

B Which is hardest for you:
Anger?
Worries? Sadness?

C Describe an outdoor activity that helps you to feel good and relaxed.

D Describe an indoor activity that makes you feel good and relaxed.

E What is something you do with your hands that helps you to feel better?

F Tell about a time that you did an enjoyable thing by yourself for too long.

HEADS

ASK YOURSELF!

If you get a heads when you flip the coin, *you* must answer one of the squares on this page.

G Describe what you usually do between waking up and lunchtime on Saturdays.

H Describe what you usually do during the afternoon and evening on Saturdays.

I Aside from your parents and teachers, who else might help you learn new ways to feel better?

J Tell about a time that you were able to help someone else feel better when they were upset.

K Describe one feel-good activity you do that you should probably cut down on.

L Of all the ways to feel good taught in this book, name two that seem most important to you.

M Describe a good way to feel better that you learned from a grown-up.

N Describe one new way to feel good that you ought to try to do more.

CHALLENGE GAME

F
When you need to calm yourself down, what is something you like to think about?

E
When your body feels hyper and restless, what are good things you can do to feel better?

D
Tell about a time that adults made you do something hard but it turned out okay later.

C
Describe what your body feels like when you are very angry.

B
What is something you have learned about calming down in the past year or two?

A
Describe something you have learned about yourself so far from reading this book.

G
Tell about a time a place seemed too loud or too crowded. How did you deal with this?

TAILS

H
Count the number of hours you spend on Sundays using computers or video games.

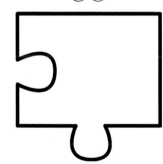

ASK SOMEONE ELSE!

If you get tails when you flip the coin, *the person to your left* must answer a question you choose from this page! (Or *the other player* if there are just two of you.)

N
Tell about a time you did something or said something that helped someone feel better.

M
What is something nice that you are looking forward to in the next month or so?

L
What is the most relaxing place in your home? What do you like to do there?

K
Ask the adult with you to show you, for one minute, how to do relaxation breathing.

J
Tell about a way to calm down and relax you should start doing more.

I
Tell about something you love that you should do less because it takes too much time.